$12.95
$4.50

D0864097

For the Birds

By Margaret Atwood
Illustrated by John Bianchi

Boxes
and sidebars
written by
Shelley Tanaka

Douglas & McIntyre
Toronto/Vancouver

Text copyright © 1990 by O.W. Toad Ltd.
Illustrations copyright © 1990 by John Bianchi

All rights reserved. No part of this book may be
reproduced or transmitted in any form by any
means without permission in writing from the
publisher, except by a reviewer, who may quote
brief passages in a review.

Douglas & McIntyre
585 Bloor Street West
Toronto, Ontario M6G 1K5

Canadian Cataloguing in Publication Data

Atwood, Margaret, 1939-
   For the birds

(Earthcare books)
ISBN 0-88894-825-5

1. Birds — Ecology — Juvenile literature.
2. Habitat (Ecology) — Juvenile literature.
3. Man — Influence on nature — Juvenile
literature.
4. Creative activities and seat work — Juvenile
literature. I. Bianchi, John. II. Title. III.
Series.

QL676.2.A88 1990   j598.25   C90-094477-3

With special thanks to Doug McRae, Long Point
Bird Observatory, Port Rowan, Ontario

Design by Michael Solomon
Printed and bound in Hong Kong

Contents

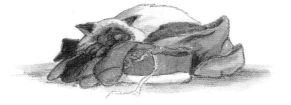

1

For the Birds

On Saturday, Samantha got out of the wrong side of bed. She knew it was the wrong side, because it was the side where she had stuffed her dirty socks and T-shirt the night before, instead of putting them into the laundry hamper. Her cat Furball had made a nest in them. Samantha stepped on the T-shirt and socks; she stepped on Furball, too.

Furball scratched Samantha's leg and went screeowling out of the room, and ran into Samantha's father. In fact she ran *up* Samantha's father, as if he were a tree. Samantha's father plucked Furball off himself like a burr and said, "Samantha, you have been getting into trouble again."

"All I did was get out of bed," said Samantha grumpily.

"On the wrong side, I guess," said her father. "Here. Take your dim-witted cat."

"She's not dim-witted," said Samantha.

"All cats are dim-witted," said her father, teasing her. "Useless, too. All cats are *for the birds*." This was what he said when he meant that a thing was silly.

That was only the beginning. At breakfast, Samantha failed to pour her milk entirely onto her cereal. She'd been trying to make a milk waterfall, but missed. This was fine with Furball, who was lurking under the table as usual to catch the

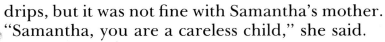

drips, but it was not fine with Samantha's mother. "Samantha, you are a careless child," she said.

After breakfast, Samantha offered to sweep the kitchen floor, to make up for things. She swept very hard; in fact, she swept so hard that the broom handle got away from her and knocked a vase of flowers off the kitchen counter which shattered into a hundred pieces on the floor. Samantha's mother sighed. "You really must learn to think before you act," she said. "*I'll* clean this up. You go outside to play. And tie your shoelaces!"

Samantha went out into the backyard. Furball went with her, and began stalking dry leaves.

"Play," thought Samantha gloomily. "How am I supposed to play? I don't have any friends here. There's nothing to do and nowhere to go, and

that stuck-up Kerry from across the street won't even speak to me."

Samantha's whole family had just moved to this house. Before, they'd lived in a small town where she knew everybody and everybody knew her, and she could walk all over town, and throw stones into the river to frighten the wild geese that sometimes swam around there. Now she was in a new house in a big city, and she wasn't even supposed to go around the block by herself. Samantha was homesick. "I wish we could move back," she said to Furball. She sat down on the edge of the back deck, feeling sorry for herself.

But then she heard some strange noises: first some squawks, then some peeping and chirping. The sounds were coming from next door. There was a high board fence between Samantha's back-

The Name Game

If one bird looks just like another to us, if we can't identify different species, how will we ever notice when one is in trouble?

See if you can name and identify ten different kinds of birds that live near your home. How about ten local animals, trees and plants?

yard and the backyard next door, but one of the boards was loose. Samantha crept up to it, moved the board to one side, and peeked through.

What she saw was a little old lady with white feathery hair, a long beaky nose, small friendly eyes and tiny claw-like hands, wearing an odd wispy black cloak over her shoulders. The squawking and peeping were coming from her! While she squawked, she was scattering birdseed on the ground, and many different kinds of birds were flying down to feed. Samantha even knew the names of some of them: a Blue Jay, a Cardinal. Samantha knew the name of the little old lady, too, because a letter for her had come to Samantha's house by mistake. Her name was Ms. Phoebe Merganser, and, watching her, Samantha decided that she was just as weird as her name.

"She is *really* for the birds," Samantha thought to herself. "What a nut-case!"

After a minute, Phoebe Merganser walked back towards her house. Samantha pulled the loose board to one side and crept into the garden. Furball crept, too. Samantha was pretending to be a hunter, sneaking up on the birds. Probably this was what Furball was thinking about as well.

As part of the game, Samantha picked up a stone and heaved it at the birds. She didn't really mean to hit one—she just wanted to see them all fly up, the way the wild geese used to—but the beautiful red Cardinal fell over onto the ground. The rest of the birds flew screaming into the trees.

Samantha didn't feel too happy. She had a sinking feeling in her stomach, like the one she'd had when the vase broke. She went over to the bird—was it dead? She was about to pick it up, when a tiny claw-like hand gripped her shoulder.

"You have hurt one of my birds," said Phoebe Merganser. Her shiny eyes did not look friendly anymore. They looked angry.

"I didn't mean to hurt it," said Samantha.

"That's what they always say when they poison rivers where the birds fish, and chop down trees where they live. You human beings are always doing careless, destructive things, and then being sorry afterwards."

Samantha had a stubborn streak. She felt her chin going out. Here she'd apologized, and she was still getting bawled out! "That's for the birds," she said rudely. "And so are you!"

Phoebe Merganser stared at her, and Samantha stared back. In fact she found she could not look away. Phoebe Merganser's eyes were getting smaller and rounder and shinier; her nose was turning into a beak, her hair and cloak into black feathers. She was changing into a bird!

Samantha opened her mouth to scream, but what came out did not sound like her own voice at all! "Eeef! Eeef!" she heard herself saying. She

Bird Language

Birds use their voices more often than any animal except for human beings. Birds call to tell other birds of food or danger, and many birds, mainly males, also sing to attract a mate and warn other birds to stay out of their territory. Baby birds learn to sing by imitating adult birds, the same way humans learn to talk.

Experienced bird-watchers can identify birds by their voices alone, without seeing them. Find out whether your local library has tapes of bird songs, which you can borrow to learn how to recognize the different songs and calls.

Crows

Crows are shiny black birds that can be as long as 45 centimetres (17 inches). They live in all parts of the world except New Zealand. Many experts think they are the most intelligent of all birds. (Scarecrows may keep some birds out of a farmer's field, but they hardly ever fool a crow!) They are also quite fearless. They have strong sharp bills that can eat pretty much anything—from corn and insects to young birds and eggs. Jays, magpies and ravens are also members of the crow family. Some people think crows make good pets, and some have even been taught to speak a few words, like parrots.

turned to run, and found herself hopping across the grass on spindly legs. She looked down at her feet just in time to see the last of her shoelaces disappear. Instead of two shoes, she now had two black bird feet. Her arms flapped, but they weren't arms, they were wings, and she didn't know how to use them. She tripped and sprawled on the lawn, an indignant heap of feathers.

"You've changed me into a bird!" she screamed at Phoebe Merganser. It was bird language, but she found she could understand it.

"And a very good thing, too," said Phoebe, who was now a large black crow. "Maybe now you'll learn something."

"Such as what?" screeched Samantha, who was mad but also scared.

"Such as a different point of view," said Phoebe Merganser. "There's more than one, you know. Maybe you'll learn what it really is like, *for the birds*."

2

Cats!

Samantha picked herself up, balancing on her new bird legs, and looked around her with her quick bird eyes. Her heart was beating quickly, as birds' hearts do. She was alert to danger. Every bush, every shadow might conceal an enemy.

Everything was so much bigger! The trees were immense, and the flowers were way over her head. She could see details that she never would have noticed before. For instance, a big shiny beetle was crawling in the grass near her feet. Before she could think what she was doing, she had snapped it up and swallowed it.

"Phnew! Gak! I just ate a beetle!" she spluttered.

"Good," said Phoebe Merganser. "Have another. You can follow it up with a few grubs, worms and caterpillars."

"Not on your life!" said Samantha indignantly, "I wouldn't be caught dead eating those things!" Although she had the body of a bird, she still had her own brain, and the idea of eating worms did not appeal to her. But she was getting hungry. She could use a bowl of Cheerios and milk right about now.

"Well, dead is what you'll be if you don't keep eating," said Phoebe Merganser cheerfully. "Birds burn up energy at a great rate. If they don't eat constantly, they'll die of starvation. That's why birds such as flycatchers, swallows and martins are such a great help keeping down mosquitoes and other pests."

"Couldn't I start on something a little less wiggly?" asked Samantha.

"Since you're a Scarlet Tanager, and Scarlet Tanagers are omnivorous—that means that they can eat just about everything that's food—I suggest you try a few seeds and dried berries from the birdfeeder tray over there," said Phoebe Merganser.

Samantha followed her advice. Getting up to the birdfeeder was hard—she didn't have control of her wings yet, so she had to flounder up onto

a low tree branch, then up to a higher one, and jump down onto the feeder—but she made it eventually. She found she could crack the seeds with her beak and swallow them down easily.

Beside the bird feeder was a fountain. Water ran down over some rocks into a shallow basin. Several small birds, chickadees and House Finches, were bathing in the fountain, splashing the water over their backs and fluffing out their feathers. They were cheeping with pleasure, just like small children squealing in a wading pond. It looked so delightful that Samantha thought she'd try, too.

She fluttered down from the birdfeeder, but lost control of her glide and made a heavy splash landing. The other birds flew off. She heard Phoebe Merganser laughing at her in Crow. Samantha stood up in the water, smouldering. But now that she was here she would have her bath anyway. She splashed herself all over and finished with a few sips from the basin. "First time I ever drank bath water," she grumbled to herself.

Now she was hungry again. Below, on the ground, was the fattest worm she had ever seen. It was also the most delicious-looking. This was the first time she'd ever thought of a worm as delicious-looking in any way. "Look at all that protein, stuffed into a handy dinner-shaped package," she thought. "A living sausage! Worm, you're worm history!"

She launched herself off the birdfeeder and pounced on the worm. In an instant it had slithered down her throat. "That wasn't so bad," she thought. "At least it didn't have any yucky legs. And I didn't have to chew it."

She was getting ready to eat another one when a movement off to one side made her turn her

Making a Birdbath

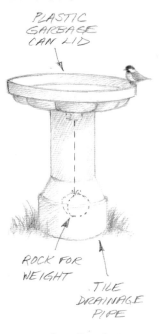

PLASTIC GARBAGE CAN LID

ROCK FOR WEIGHT

TILE DRAINAGE PIPE

Put a birdbath in your backyard. You can use the upside-down lid of a plastic garbage can, or a shallow pan (try not to use tin, which can get very hot when the sun is shining). The water should be no more than 5 centimetres (2 inches) deep, and it should be changed every couple of days. If you have cats, put the birdbath out in the open so your cats can't sneak up on the birds.

What Birds Eat

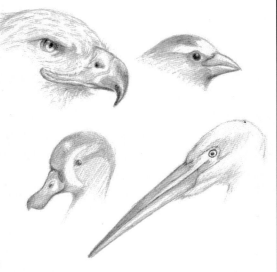

Some birds, including hawks and owls, are carnivorous; they eat meat—snakes, mice, small birds and large insects. These birds have strong hooked beaks for tearing up flesh. Herbivorous birds eat mainly seeds and grasses. They have short thick bills for crushing seeds. Other birds are omnivorous; they eat insects and plants. These birds often have slender pointed beaks for picking up caterpillars, beetles and other crawling insects. Ducks and other water birds have broad flat beaks with serrated edges for straining food from water.

head. Just in time! Flying at her through the air was a monster! It had fiery yellow eyes, huge sharp claws, a mouthful of evil fang-shaped teeth, and it was covered all over with horrible bristly fur!

"Yikes! Yikes! Yikes!" she screamed. She leapt backwards and took off. She was in the air and flying before she knew it.

She landed on a handy low branch and began to scold. "Cat! Cat! Cat!" she yelled, warning any other bird within hearing distance. Then she peered more closely.

The cat was Furball, her own warm and cuddly pussycat! Furball looked quite different and a lot more sinister, now that Samantha was a bird.

"Furball, you stupid turkey!" she said. "I was almost lunch! Don't you know me? And anyway, you've already had your disgusting mushy Gourmet Cat Food today! I dished it out myself!

Furball flattened herself on the grass and peered up, switching her tail. Obviously she did not understand Scarlet Tanager. But then, she'd never been very good at Human, either.

Phoebe Merganser flew down to perch on a nearby branch. "Narrow escape," she remarked. "Birds learn fast, or else. You don't usually get a second chance, with cats."

"Why do they let those vicious killers roam around free?" Samantha complained. "All they do is yowl at night, make cat bathrooms in the flower beds and kill birds." She was remembering the various little bird corpses Furball had brought to the back door lately. She hadn't thought much about it, then.

"That's not how you felt when you were a human," said Phoebe. "Anyway, it's no use blaming the cats. Hunting is an instinct for them, and they'll do it no matter how much you feed them. But if you want to have cat pets and protect the birds, too, there are certain precautions you can take."

"Such as?" asked Samantha.

"Keep them inside at dawn and dusk, when birds feed on the ground and the light is dim; and especially at nesting time, migration time, and when young birds are leaving the nest and learning to fly. Put cat-proof collars around the trunks of trees, so cats can't get at the nests. Have your birdfeeder in the open, with perching trees around but without bushes nearby where cats can hide and sneak up. Try bells on their collars. If you're really ambitious, you can make a cat-proof fence."

"That would be all very well," grumbled Samantha, "if I were a human being. But I'm

stuck in this bird-brained bird body. How am I going to get back to normal? And what's my mom going to say when I'm not home in time for lunch?"

3

The Deadly Glass Mountain

"We'll jump that one when we come to it," said Phoebe. "Anyway, your mom and dad and your teachers are always going on about learning experiences. Right?"

"Yeah," said Samantha, ruffling her feathers. "They are. So?"

"So this *is* one! They can hardly complain. Anyway, it's time for us to start migrating. If we don't get a hop on, we'll be caught by the cold weather. We'd have to eat a lot more to keep warm, and there won't be a worm or a beetle in sight. They'll all be dead or hibernating. Let's go!"

"Let's go where?" asked Samantha. Being a Scarlet Tanager right next to her own backyard was bad enough. She didn't want to be one in some place she didn't even know.

"South America," said Phoebe Merganser. "Warm in the winter, fruits and berries you wouldn't believe, and bugs as big as your beak! Crows don't usually migrate that far, but of course I'm not exactly an ordinary crow."

"Ack! *Where?*" said Samantha. But Phoebe was already in the air. "Follow me!" she cawed. Saman-

The Migration Mystery

Scientists are still not sure why some birds migrate, or fly from one area to another at certain times of the year. We don't know exactly when migrating birds first started to migrate, or why they do it, though it's clear that they go from places where there is less food to places where there is more.

Why do birds go back to the very same nesting and feeding spots year after year, and how do they know how to get there? Experts used to think that birds steer by the stars, since many fly at night, but birds seem to know where to go even during long periods of cloudy weather. Some scientists think the earth's magnetic forces guide the birds, but no one knows for sure. It's likely that different birds use different methods to find their way, depending on the weather, time of day, etc.

How do the birds know when to fly south? The birds may migrate when the food supply starts to run out, though there is at least one species that leaves its northern home in August, just when food is the most plentiful. Some adult shorebirds fly south before their chicks, leaving behind a bigger food supply for the young birds.

And why do the birds bother returning north to breed? It may be because the long summer days in their northern habitats give the birds more hours to search for food and feed their young, but again, nobody knows for sure.

Migration's World Champion

The Arctic Tern has the longest migration trip of all birds. In August it flies from the Arctic to the Antarctic, and it returns north in mid June—a round trip of 35,000 kilometres (21,700 miles) eack year. As a result, this bird sees more daylight than any creature on earth!

tha didn't want to be out of sight of the only person who had the power to change her back to who she really was.

Also the only person who could understand her: the other birds seemed to think she was a bird like them, and if they thought that, so would the humans. Even her own family. If she tried to fly into her house, they'd probably think she had lice or something. She remembered what had happened to a stray bat that got in once. Her mother had run around blithering, with a towel over her head to keep the bat from getting into her hair; her father had whacked it out of the air with a tennis racquet; Furball had jumped it, and that was Farewell Bat.

"It's going to be Farewell Samantha unless I catch up with that Phoebe Merganser," thought Samantha. "Here goes nothing."

She launched herself off the tree branch into the air and soon caught up with Phoebe, who'd been doing a slow circle, waiting for her.

"Won't the other birds think it's kind of weird, a Scarlet Tanager migrating with a crow?" she asked. She'd watched geese migrating; in their formations, it was all geese.

"Well, it is a bit out of the ordinary," said Phoebe. "But many birds migrate in mixed flocks."

"Why do they do that?" asked Samantha.

"Who knows?" said Phoebe. "Safety in numbers, I guess. There are a lot of things about birds we still don't know. Migration itself is still a mystery."

"How do they know the way?" asked Samantha. She herself knew how to tell the directions on a map, but birds had no maps.

Birdathons

Every year, Long Point Bird Observatory in Ontario, Canada, holds the Baillie Birdathon, the largest birdathon in the world.

You can organize your own birdathon. Have each member of your class find sponsors who are willing to pay a certain amount for each species of bird that you spot. Then organize a birdwatching expedition to see how many kinds of birds you can count. The money that you raise can be donated to your favourite wildlife or environmental organization.

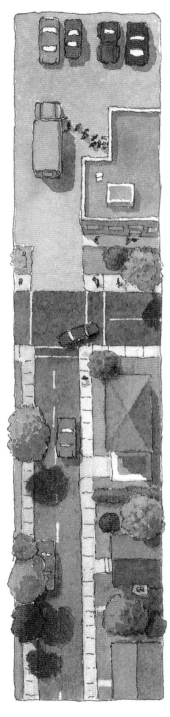

"Who can tell?" said Phoebe. "But the birds seem to know exactly where they're going. Many birds return to the same nesting areas year after year, and when they go south they return to the same feeding areas. It's like you knowing your own address—not just the area, but the house. Birds are a lot smarter than many people think they are."

The two birds had been gaining altitude as they talked, and now they were high over the city, heading south. Everything looked very different from the air. The people on the sidewalk looked like ants, the cars like beetles. From above, the trees looked like green bath sponges; some of the leaves were already turning colour. The houses looked like little building blocks, the parking lots like asphalt deserts. Samantha found it made her happy to see green backyards with trees in them that meant food for birds, and shelter. But a lot of the territory they were crossing was bad news for birds. No trees, freeways with rushing cars that would smush you as soon as look at you, and pavement and roofs where no trees or worms could grow.

Over to one side were some tall smokestacks with yellow and grey smoke belching out of them. "We try to stay clear of those," said Phoebe. "The poisonous chemicals in that smoke are a major health hazard for birds. A lot of people don't pay that much attention to it, as long as it's just killing birds. But because the smoke blows all over everything, it's turning into a major health hazard for human beings as well. The chemicals fall onto the land and get absorbed by the vegetables you eat; they fall into the water and you drink them. And of course you can breathe them in, too. What's

Birds and Their Habitats

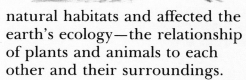

Every bird needs certain sur-roundings to survive—a special combination of the right weather, trees and plants, water, soil, sunlight, safe nesting spots and certain kinds of food. These surroundings make up the bird's habitat.

Even a small change can affect a habitat. If a tree is cut down, a bird may lose its shelter, nesting spot and food from the insects that live in the tree. Plants grow-ing beneath the tree may die without the shade from the tree's leaves. These shade plants may have been home to rodents and insects that larger predators relied on for food. Or perhaps the rich top layer of soil that was held in place by the tree's roots will now be washed away.

A change in the environment can also affect something far away. If a river is dammed, for instance, water birds that live far downstream can lose their source of food, water and shelter.

Every change we make to the environment affects something else. Over the years, our factories and cars and garbage have pol-luted the air and the water. Our buildings and parking lots and highways have paved over many natural habitats and affected the earth's ecology—the relationship of plants and animals to each other and their surroundings.

It is time we stopped harming the environment, and time we started making special places for birds and other wildlife, to replace a few of the ones we have taken away.

One of the best ways to help is by letting the people in charge know that you want things to change. If you would like to see a cemetery turned into a bird habitat, or hunting laws changed, or spraying stopped in your local park, find out the name of the person in charge by looking in your phone book, calling your public library or your local envi-ronmental group, or asking your teachers or parents for help. Then write a letter telling the authori-ties what you want changed, and why. Make sure you put your address on the letter, and ask the person to write you back. Send a copy of the letter to your mayor or government leader, and ask them to write you back, too.

Jungles in the City

Cities and towns can have special spots for birds, too. Some cities have set up "natural" parks—small wild areas where plants and trees are allowed to grow naturally to attract birds and add a bit of wilderness to the asphalt desert. If you have an empty lot in your neighbourhood, find out who owns it. Ask the owners to turns it into a natural park. Write to your mayor and city council and tell them you would like to have wilderness areas in your city.

bad for the birds will be bad for people, sooner or later. The old miners knew that. They used to take a canary in a cage down into the mines with them. If the canary keeled over, it meant there were poisonous gases around. When you're in a place where the air is killing the birds, it's going to get you, too, if you don't look out."

"So why do those people keep putting poisons into the air?" asked Samantha.

"Greed," said Phoebe. "They think it would cost them too much money to clean up their act."

"That's not too smart, is it?" said Samantha.

"Nope," said Phoebe. "And up ahead, you'll see something else that's not too smart."

Samantha looked. They were passing the central area of the city. Many high towers of glass glittered in the sun.

"Those are just high-rises," she said. "Downtown office buildings. They've got stores at the bottom. What's so bad about them?"

"Well," said Phoebe, "when the birds are migrating by night, and all the lights are left on, the birds get confused. They smash into the glass and get murdered."

"Murdered?" said Samantha.

"If they were people you'd call it murder," said Phoebe. "Criminal negligence, at the very least."

"I see what you mean," said Samantha. She was imagining what it would be like to smash into a glass tower at high speed in the middle of the night.

But now that they were coasting along through the air and she had a little time to think, she was also wondering about Phoebe herself.

"May I ask you a question?" she said after a moment. "Are you a bird who's really a little old

lady, or are you a little old lady who's really a
bird?"

"Are you a girl who's really a nosy brat, or
are you a nosy brat who's really a girl?" Phoebe
answered sulkily. She clamped her bill shut and
refused to say anything more. Maybe she was
annoyed at being called "little" and "old." Come
to think of it, that wasn't too polite. If she'd had
her girl's face on, Samantha would have blushed.

4

The Dying Duck

Bad News for Birds

If you live in an area where roads are salted in winter, write to the government department in charge of your highways and ask whether sand could be used instead. Road salt is bad news for birds. Not only does it damage nearby trees and plants, but many winter birds gather to feed on the salt and are killed by cars.

When Phoebe had stopped being mad, she explained to Samantha that although they had almost reached the shore of Lake Ontario, they were not going to fly south right over it. "I want to show you a bit more of the countryside," she said. "Anyway, small birds prefer not to fly straight across large bodies of open water, except when they really have to. Ducks and seagulls and such don't mind it, because they can swim and fish, but we aren't those kinds of birds. We'll go the Lake Erie route; down there, we can island-hop."

Since Samantha had no idea where they were going anyway, she had no objections. But she was getting hungry again. "When do we eat?" she said. If she were still a little girl, she'd be looking out the car window for a hamburger place right about now.

"Keep your eyes peeled. We need a patch of woods, or a likely-looking backyard," said Phoebe. "How about right down there?"

They drifted in for a landing, near a big brick house with some useful trees around it. "One of those trees is an apple tree," said Phoebe. "You might find some good stuff there. Scarlet Tanagers are very fond of fruit-tree pests, which is why farmers with orchards should encourage them."

"What about you?" said Samantha. "Care to join me?"

"I see a yummy squashed mouse by the roadside over there," said Phoebe. "Crows are scavengers, among other things, and we eat roadkill. You've probably seen us doing it when you were a little girl going out for a drive."

"Yuck! So that's what you were doing," said Samantha. "Excuse me while I throw up."

"Don't be so high and mighty," said Phoebe. "If crows and ravens and vultures didn't eat dead animals, who'd clean them up? Not you, Miss Smarty Pants!"

Samantha thought about that as she hopped about in the apple tree on the front lawn, looking for grubs and beetles. But suddenly a stone whizzed by her head, and then another one! Then a small pellet! With a squawk she flew up into the air. She heard laughter. It was coming from three or four boys, and one of them had an airgun!

Luckily she knew what that was. She flew off to find Phoebe Merganser, just as the boy was taking aim again.

"Those idiot boys!" she spluttered. "They almost killed me!"

"So what else is new?" said Phoebe. "Boys will be boys. Anyway, they think it's fun. And as I recall, boys aren't the only kind of humans who behave like that."

Samantha remembered her own stone-throwing habits, and hung her head in shame.

By late afternoon Samantha was about ready to drop. "We need to look for a good place to roost," said Phoebe. "How about over there by the edge of that swamp? Cats don't like swimming, as a rule, so if we can roost in a tree that's surrounded by water we'll at least be safe from them!"

Samantha remembered the time she had decided to give Furball a bath. Furball had stuck all her fur straight up on end and spread out her feet, trying to hang on to all four sides of the bathtub at once. The noises she'd made were unearthly. Samantha's mother had came running into the bathroom, saying, "Why are you torturing that cat?" Samantha had had some fairly bad scratches afterwards.

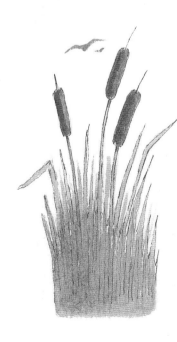

"Sounds like a good idea to me," she said.

They landed beside the swamp and began to feed. But as they were eating, they heard a mournful quacking sound from behind a clump of bulrushes. Samantha found that she could understand Duck speech, as well as Crow. This duck was saying, "Alack! Alack! Quack, quack, alack!"

"Let's see what's wrong," she said to Phoebe.

The two of them flew cautiously around the bulrushes.

Two Mallard Ducks were sitting on a floating log. One of them, the male, looked very ill, his eyes were half-closed, his feathers were dull, and he seemed exhausted. The female was anxiously preening his neck feathers; it was she who had been making the unhappy sounds.

"What's the matter?" asked Samantha.

"This is my mate, this is my mate," said the duck. "It was something he ate, it was something he ate. Oh, dreadful fate! Too late, too late, too late, too late!"

Ducks, Samantha decided, had a habit of repeating themselves. "What was it that he ate?" she asked.

"Lead, lead, lead! And now he'll soon be dead, dead, dead!" wailed the female duck.

Samantha remembered tales she'd heard about little children who had come to bad ends from sucking lead pencils, back when they used to put lead in pencils. Lead in your body made you stupid, and that was only the beginning. She also remembered things she'd heard on the news, about lead poisoning in the air, from factories, and how people had tried to stop it. She'd seen a T-shirt once with "GET THE LEAD OUT" on it. But ducks didn't eat old-fashioned lead pencils or hang around factories!

"Why the heck would he be eating lead?" she asked.

"Oh woe, don't you know?" wept the female duck. "It's in the shot, it's in the hot shot, it's in the no-fun guns the hunters use for taking a pot-shot! You have no idea what it's like, being a duck! Or maybe you do. What do they yell at you when

a baseball's coming your way and it's about to hit you on the head?"

"Duck," said Samantha.

"Right," said the duck. "And that's what we're always doing. Ducking! Everywhere we go, especially during hunting season! Fall migration used to be bad enough, but now it's ridiculous! Blam! Blam! Blam! A bunch of men in funny hats, hiding in little huts, luring us down with wooden decoys, then blazing away at us with both barrels! Some of us get killed outright. Others are wounded, and the lead in the shot poisons them! And if you escape that—oh, what bad luck, being a duck! You're minding your own business, upended and dabbling in the mud at the bottom of a pond, and by mistake you eat the lead shot from all those guns, which falls into the water and sinks! The swamps and ponds are filling up with lead, lead, lead, and soon we'll all be dead, dead, dead! And then people wonder why there are fewer and fewer of us each year! Oh, dear, oh, dear!"

"That's awful!" said Samantha. "Can't anyone get them to stop it? Can't you *tell* them?

"They aren't listening," said Phoebe grimly. "There are some parks where hunting is forbidden and the ducks are safe. But even if they don't get hit, they can't be protected from eating lead shot. Also, the lead gradually dissolves and works its way into the water that people drink. And when you consider the lead that comes out the backs of cars because of leaded gasoline, it all adds up to too much lead! Who knows how many people are suffering from lead poisoning right now, and don't even know it?"

"They'll see, they'll see," said the duck. "They'll end up just like my mate and me! What did we ever do to them? Oh, misery!"

"I'm really sorry," said Samantha. She didn't know what else to say.

"It's kind of you to mind," said the duck. "Goodbye, goodbye! And when you fly, far away into the southern sky, remember me and my mate, and our sad fate. Oh, too late, too late, too late!"

Hunting

Irresponsible hunting can destroy an entire bird or animal population. Shooting nearly wiped out the North American Whooping Cranes; in France, after the French Revolution, laws preventing hunting were ignored, and so many birds were killed that insects, rats and mice began to destroy farm crops.

Find out about hunting in your area. Does your government know how many birds or animals are caught, and whether any species are in danger of being wiped out? Are there laws that control hunting, such as outlawing hunting when birds or animals are breeding, or that restrict the number of creatures that are killed?

5

The Bird Motel

The next day Phoebe and Samantha continued to head south. They didn't follow the roads, because they didn't have to. They cut across country. "You've heard the saying, '*As the crow flies?*'" said Phoebe. "It means, *In a straight line*. No traffic jams for us!" Nothing very bad happened to them, except that Phoebe was chased by a flock of Red-winged Blackbirds who did not like crows, and Samantha was almost pounced on by a hawk.

"You've heard the saying, *Dog eat dog*?" said Phoebe. "Well, with some birds it's *Bird eat bird*."

"You have a lot of sayings," said Samantha. "Sort of like my dad."

Thinking about her dad made her feel sad. Being a bird was exciting, and she was glad she'd learned how to fly—but when was she going to see her home again, and her parents, and Furball? Was she ever going to regain her girl shape? Birds don't cry, so Samantha didn't. But she felt lonely.

"Look down there!" cried Phoebe encouragingly. "Now we're getting somewhere!"

Below them was a small town, and as they swooped down towards it, Samantha could see a large banner strung across the main street: WELCOME TO THE FALL MIGRATION!

"Now that's appreciation," said Phoebe.

"Do they think birds can read?" said Samantha.

"The sign isn't for the birds," said Phoebe. "It's for the birders."

Wildlife Sanctuaries

Most countries have wildlife refuges and nature reserves—places where hunting is banned and plants and wildlife are supposed to be left undisturbed. But even these wilderness areas can be threatened. Some governments are allowing sport hunting, mining, trapping, logging and hydro-electric development in parks and reserves.

Find out who is in charge of your country's wildlife sanctuaries. Write and let them know that you want wilderness areas to be left wild.

"The what?" asked Samantha.

"A birder is a person who enjoys watching birds," said Phoebe. "Although there aren't any playoffs and you can't watch it on TV, birding is now the largest sport in North America. All kinds of people do it—old ones, young ones, men, women, everyone. Some people even do it in wheelchairs."

Samantha thought about this. If a person who watched birds was a birder, what was a person who watched cats? A catter? And did you call it *catting*?

"Why do they do it here, in particular?" asked Samantha.

"We're near Lake Erie now," said Phoebe. "A lot of birds pass this way in the spring and fall. They travel down Point Pelee, which is a national park, so at least they're safe from being shot at.

Becoming a Birder

A lot of nature lovers begin their careers by birdwatching. You don't need to be an expert to watch birds, and you can observe them whether you live in the country or the city. You can go birdwatching on your own, or with one or two friends. You don't need any special equipment, either, though it helps to carry a notebook and a pencil.

The easiest way to begin your birdwatching career is to find a quiet spot outdoors—in your yard, in a park, in a cemetery, or on a quiet road. Sit down, and wait. It shouldn't be long before a bird comes your way.

Now, watch the bird.

• What colour is it? What marks does it have, and where are they—on the breast, wings, head or tailfeathers?
• How big is the bird? The size of a robin or a starling? A sparrow? A crow? What is the shape of its beak and its head?
• What is the bird doing? Is it on the ground or flying? What is it eating? Does it hop or walk? How does it fly—in a straight line or in a pattern? What sound does it make?
• Finally, where is the bird? In a city? Near water? A field? Is it near evergreen trees or deciduous?
• What season is it, and what is the weather like? What time of day is it?

Write down what you see in a notebook. Better yet, sketch the bird. Even if you think you can't draw, sketching will make you think about what you are observing. (Imagine that each bird is wearing its own uniform, complete with its distinctive bars, blotches and stripes.) Later, you can look in bird guides to help you identify the bird.

The more you find out, the more exciting birdwatching will be. Soon you will be able to do more than tell a chickadee from a sparrow; you may be able to tell one chickadee from another!

Endangered Birds

Right now, there are over 8,000 different species of birds in the world. But human carelessness is causing birds, plants and animals to disappear every day. And once a creature is extinct, nothing can be done to bring it back.

If we work together, we can change things. The Whooping Crane, for instance, used to be widespread in North America, until shooting and habitat destruction killed off almost all of them. By 1941, only 15 were known to exist in the wild, and experts thought the bird would soon be extinct. But since then, Canadian and American wildlife services have worked to build up the population of these birds, by breeding them and releasing them into the wild, and by making it illegal to hunt them. Now there are more than 150 Whooping Cranes.

The Bald Eagle, White-tailed Eagle and Peregrine Falcon have all been threatened by humans. Many have been hunted by people who think the birds kill livestock (in fact, these birds mainly eat animals that are already dead). And the poisons in pesticides have worked their way through the food chain into the fish that these birds eat, making the birds unable to hatch healthy young.

Now efforts are being made to save these birds before it's too late. The most harmful pesticides and hunting have been banned. Young birds have been raised in captivity and released into the wild. And wildlife groups are trying to protect the birds' nesting sites and restore their habitat. But the battle is not over yet. The Peregrine Falcon, for example, is still considered an endangered species in many parts of the world. And new dangers, such as acid rain, may be just as harmful as pesticides.

Find out about endangered species—perhaps a bird or animal that is native to your area. Write to your local wildlife authorities. Learn what is being done about saving these creatures, and ask what you can do to help.

Point Pelee is triangular, and it sticks out into the water. It's sort of like a funnel: a lot of birds come from all directions into the big end of the triangle, and then they fly from the small end, so they're closer together and you can see more of them at once. In spring it's the reverse; they land on the small end. They make the big flight across the lake using a chain of limestone islands. In ancient times those islands were a land bridge; that must have been when the birds established their custom of crossing there."

"I see a lot of Purple Martin houses," Samantha said, "and a lot of birdfeeders."

"The people around here are very bird-conscious," said Phoebe. "They know the birds bring the birders, and that's good for local business. There's even some talk of turning the local cemeteries into special bird habitats."

"*Cemeteries*?" said Samantha. "Oooh. Creepy!"

"The bird is an ancient symbol for the soul," said Phoebe. "But apart from that, think about it. What's in cemeteries?"

"Creaky tombs," said Samantha. "Gravestones. Vampires. The Wives of Dracula." She had seen a lot of horror movies.

"You're still thinking like a human," said Phoebe. "Think like a bird."

"Trees and bushes," said Samantha. "Flowers, sometimes."

"And flowers mean—"

"Insects! Bugs and beetles!" said Samantha. Now she was thinking like a bird! She wanted a large beakful of the delicious little critters right now!

"So, it's not so hard to turn a cemetery into good bird habitat," said Phoebe. "It's good bird

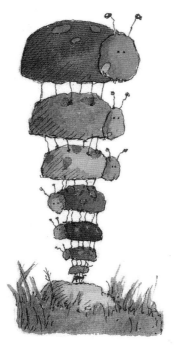

habitat already—and at least they aren't paving it over or building factories on it, not yet anyway. So all they have to do is add a nice fountain and take care to plant a variety of good bird trees, and some evergreens for shelter. Oh, yes, and get rid of any chemical pesticides and herbicides. You may think those things just kill bugs and weeds, but they get on the insects and then birds eat them. They end up in the Food Chain."

"What's that, some kind of a supermarket?" said Samantha.

"Nope. It's *everything we eat.* You've heard the saying, 'Small bugs have bigger bugs upon their backs to bite 'em, bigger bugs have bigger bugs, and so *ad infinitum*'?"

"Actually I haven't," said Samantha.

"Well, you have now," said Phoebe. "What it means is everything eats something and gets eaten

Bird Cemeteries

Visit your local cemetery. Would it make a good bird habitat? Find out who owns the cemetery and ask the owners to put up a birdbath and plant shrubs and trees to attract birds and provide them with shelter. (The trees and shrubs should be species that grow naturally in the area.) If the owners spray the cemetery to keep it free from bugs or weeds, ask them to stop. See whether your school or community group can help turn the cemetery into a special place for birds.

by something, which gets eaten by something else, and so on forever. And if some of those things get poisoned, the poison is passed along the Food Chain, until it ends up . . ."

"In double-decker hamburgers with tomato, cheese and relish and a side of fries," said Samantha gloomily.

"That's the big picture," said Phoebe. "But some people don't get it. They still spray for mosquitoes, and . . ."

"Stop right there," said Samantha. "Who likes getting bitten by mosquitoes? Not me!"

"Not me, either," said Phoebe. "But spraying them is like using an atom bomb to kill a mouse, because that kind of spraying kills a lot of other things besides the mosquitoes. Try encouraging bats and Purple Martins in your neighbourhood, and wearing protective clothing and using an

Battling the Bugs

There are safe ways to discourage biting insects. Different things work for different people, so try them all.
- *Wear loose clothing, and avoid dark colours (some experts say that mosquitoes are especially fond of reds and blues).*
- *Keep your collars and sleeves tightly closed. Tuck your shirt in firmly, and tuck your trousers into your boots, or pull your socks up over the trouser cuffs.*
- *Try using citronella as an insect repellant. It is an oil extracted from citrus fruits, and can be bought in drugstores.*
- *Some people have found that eating lots of garlic and avoiding refined sugar keeps the bugs away.*

insect repellant. There's a safe one you can make yourself. A lot of birders are using it, and if anyone knows about mosquitoes, they do. They're always crawling around in swamps. Now, let's head for the Bird Motel."

"Bird Motel?" said Samantha. "Is that for birders, too?"

"No. This time it's for the birds," said Phoebe. "Actually it's called Robertson's Healthi-Gro Organic Farm. But we birds call it the Bird Motel. And do the Robertsons ever love birds! They know who keeps their cabbage worms and their slugs and aphids under control! Everything there is top grade—no poisons in the carrots and cabbages they grow, and no poisons in the insects you can pick up there for a song! Worms you could die for! Believe me, it's the best place to eat around here!"

Samantha had to agree. She hadn't eaten so well in days. The best of everything, with a cool shower in the Robertsons' birdbath thrown in. At dusk she nestled in the branches of a thick red cedar tree, listening to the distant hooting of the owls who were hunting mice in the Robertsons' fields. Even the Robertsons' mice would be good for you, she thought drowsily. She fell asleep and dreamed she was in a supermarket with shelves filled with food, and big signs above them:

FOOD CHAIN BARGAINS!
Beetles. Grade A, Guaranteed Pesticide-Free.
Today's Special: Scrumptious Slugs.
Owl Treat! Organic Mice: 2.00/doz.

Maybe I'm turning into a bird completely, she said to herself when she woke up. *Maybe I'm losing my human mind. This is not what I used to think of as a beautiful dream!*

Plant a Bird Garden

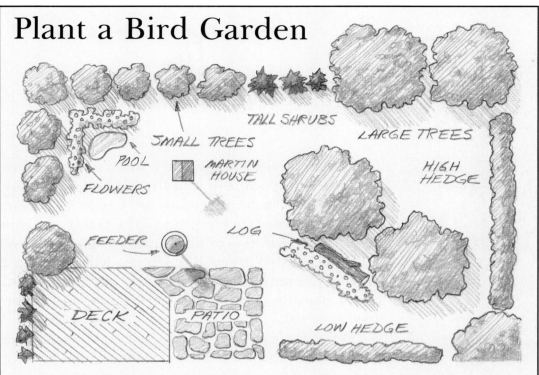

POOL

FLOWERS

SMALL TREES

TALL SHRUBS

MARTIN HOUSE

LARGE TREES

HIGH HEDGE

LOG

FEEDER

DECK

PATIO

LOW HEDGE

Plant a bird garden, perhaps in a corner of your schoolyard. You can grow flowers, shrubs and trees that will produce seeds and fruits that birds like to eat. Try to plant shrubs and trees of different heights, including low shrubs, ground covers and trees. Plants with thorns will provide some protection from cats. For a simple bird garden, throw grass and wildflower seed on the ground and let it grow. And let your garden stay a little messy—don't mow the grass, and let leaves and grass stalks stay on the ground to provide nesting materials.

Let flowers go to seed. Throw a decayed log or two in to attract burrowing insects.

Or, for the easiest bird garden of all, make a brushpile. Just gather dead sticks and branches and pile them on top of each other. Keep adding to the pile when more branches fall off existing trees—the bigger the pile, the better. These piles will provide excellent cover for birds.

Find out what plants, bushes and trees grow naturally in your area. They will attract the most birds.

6

The Vampire Forest

The next day they made it across Lake Erie, from one limestone island to another. They saw many seagulls, and a large colony of Cormorants on some dead trees sticking out of the water. By this time the air was full of migrating birds—flocks of swallows, Red-Winged Blackbirds, Killdeers, and warblers of many kinds. For days they flew south. It got warmer, and there were more and more insects to eat.

"Why don't we just stop here?" said Samantha one day, as they were flying over a dark-looking forest.

"First, it's not your winter habitat," said Phoebe. "Birds are very traditional, you know. They hate ending up in the wrong place. Second, we're only down as far as the southern United States. They get winter, too. They may not get snow and ice, but it turns cold and the leaves fall off a lot of the trees, and the insects die or hibernate. You wouldn't make out very well. And third—and this is important—that place down there is known as the Vampire Forest. It's best to keep right out of it!"

"The Vampire Forest!" said Samantha with a shudder. She looked at the forest again. It was all pine trees, row upon row of them. It did look gloomy. "What do you mean? Are there vampires down there?"

"No," said Phoebe, laughing as much as a crow can laugh. "The forest itself is a vampire. In folktales, vampires were once known as the Undead. They were thought to be creatures who were neither alive nor dead; they kept themselves going by drinking the blood of living creatures. This forest is the same. It's not exactly alive, but it isn't dead, either. And it's kept alive by the blood of the living."

"How come?" said Samantha. The more she stared at them, the creepier those trees down there looked!

"A long time ago now," said Phoebe, "when people started cutting down trees in the fir and pine forests, they realized that sometimes the forests got hit badly by certain kinds of insects. A whole lot of these insects would appear at once, and they would eat all the needles or bark or buds of the trees, and the trees could die. Insects such as sawflies and spruce budworm, for instance. If the trees died and then stood around, pretty soon they were no good for lumber and such.

"Then people invented something they thought would save the forests. They invented insect sprays, and they went around in little planes, spraying huge doses of these poisonous insecticides onto the trees. The sprays did kill the harmful insects; trouble is, they killed many other insects, too. Birds ate the poisonous insects and were poisoned. Some died, and some lost the ability to lay eggs that would hatch.

"And the sprays didn't kill *all* the harmful insects. Some of them survived and developed a resistance to the sprays. That means the poisons no longer poison them. They become Superbugs. And they keep on making more and more harmful

Logging

Once a forest has been completely cut down, it will never be the same again. Even if new trees are planted, the same songbirds and animals that lived in the uncut forest may not return.

Find out how trees are logged in your country. Do the loggers cut rows or small areas and then allow the cut areas to grow back naturally from the seeds of surroundings trees? Or do they cut down entire forests and then try to plant new trees? How many new trees are planted? How many of the ones that are planted survive? Is just one kind of tree planted, or several? How are logs taken out of the area, and how does this affect the environment?

insects, which keep on infesting the trees. So the sprayers keep on spraying.

"Now the people who do the spraying feel stuck. If they stop, they think the insect infestation will get out of control. But if they keep on spraying, more and more birds—and animals and fish—will die. And now they know that the sprays are very bad for the people who breathe them in, especially children. Some have even died from diseases linked to these sprays. This is why we call that forest the Vampire Forest. It's kept alive on death."

"So what can be done?" asked Samantha.

"Scientists are working on insect controls that don't involve poisons," said Phoebe. "Another way is to just let the forest run its natural cycle: let it die, let it regrow. Another way is to increase the number of insect predators—things that eat the harmful insects. These can be birds, or they can be other insects. And sometimes paper companies and logging companies will cut an insect-damaged stand of trees while they can still use the trees. But one thing is certain. Spraying for forest insects does a great deal of harm, and should be stopped as soon as possible."

"How come those trees are all in such straight rows?" said Samantha. "They almost look planted."

Phoebe cawed with laughter. "They *are* planted," she said. "That's what you might call a man-made forest. And you'll notice the trees are all one kind. When only one kind of a plant or tree is planted, that's called a *monoculture*. Monocultures aren't such hot news for bird life, either."

"How come?" asked Samantha. It did look boring down there, but she could remember being

bored when she was a girl. Boredom didn't kill you.

"One kind of tree, one kind of food," said Phoebe. "Nature prefers variety. Imagine if all people ever had to eat was sausages, and only mean-eyed red-headed boys with big feet could eat them. Soon everyone else would die out. The world would be full of nothing but mean-eyed red-headed boys with big feet."

"What a disgusting thought!" cried Samantha, who had known several boys just like that.

Luckily they were now past the Vampire Forest. Ahead of them was the coast, and beyond that gleamed the sea.

7

The Burning Desert

For days they flew south, from tree to tree, along the tropical coast of Mexico, then down into South America. The sunshine was warm and there were bright flowers; there were delicious insects Samantha had never seen before, and fruits she'd never tasted. This was wonderful! She thought about all the other kids way back up north, sitting in the schoolroom or shivering in their winter coats while she flew around down here, free as a bird.

"Phoebe," she said one day. "Will I ever get back my human shape?"

"Humph," said Phoebe. She was eating part of a banana, and her beak was full. "Wrf 'n shee."

"What?" said Samantha.

"I said, 'Wait and see.'"

"Oh," said Samantha. "Well, if I do, can I keep the wings?"

"You could, I suppose," said Phoebe. "But you wouldn't be able to fly."

"Why not?" said Samantha. She had a vision of herself swooping around the schoolyard and perching on the roof, while all the other kids' eyes bugged out with admiration and envy.

"Too heavy," said Phoebe. "Birds have hollow bones. Humans have solid ones. You'd never get off the ground."

This was a discouraging thought. When she got discouraged Samantha liked to change the subject, so she said, "When are we going to get there?"

"Where is there?" said Phoebe.

"Wherever we're going."

"We're going to your wintering ground in the rainforest jungles of the Amazon," said Phoebe. "Do you remember your geography? It's that very large green feathery-looking part on the map of South America."

"Rainforest," said Samantha. "I hope that doesn't mean it's going to rain all the time."

"Nope. But it's damp, you might say. The dampness and the heat are what make it so fertile, and so full of good things for birds to eat, and with so many branches where birds can perch. A perfect place for birds! Look ahead—that's the edge of it now!"

Samantha looked. Sure enough, up ahead was a large expanse of green. But as they flew nearer, they could see other things that were not green. Roads were being built down there, brown roads; bulldozers and tractors moved along them. On

How Birds Fly

Birds have feathers, which streamline their bodies and help them glide through the air. Birds also have very strong breast muscles to move their wings, as well as excellent eyesight, so they can change direction quickly and don't bump into branches when they are flying through trees.

Birds have no teeth, which are heavy; instead, they have light beaks and, inside their bodies, a gizzard where food is ground down. Their ears do not stick out and slow them down, but are small holes in the sides of their heads. And birds have air sacs in their bodies and hollow, slender bones that make them lighter for flying.

either side of the roads there were cleared patches that looked scorched. Dead, burnt tree trunks with no leaves on them stood like withered sticks. Beyond that, smoke was rising from among the still-green trees. The rainforest was on fire!

"What's happening down there? It's a fire! Why aren't they putting it out?" cried Samantha.

"Those fires were started by people," said Phoebe grimly. "They are clearing the land; they want to put cows there. But the soil of the rainforest is very thin. The jungle itself holds the soil in place, and when it dries out very little can grow there. Not only are they destroying bird life, they're destroying the very soil itself. And they're destroying the trees that create the oxygen we all breathe. They are making a desert."

"This is terrible!" cried Samantha. "How can

they be stopped?" She flew closer to get a better look. A huge puff of smoke spurted upwards, and she was caught by it. She coughed and spluttered and tried to fly into clean air, but the smothering grey vapour was all around her.

Her lungs were filling with smoke; she felt herself getting dizzy, she could no longer fly, she was blanking out. Now she was falling, down, down through the choking smoke towards the ground far below, where the fires were flaring red among the scorched trees. She was hurtling straight towards one of the fires! She would be burnt up, she would be nothing but a little dustball of singed feathers!

"Goodbye, world," she thought, as the flickering red patch below grew larger and larger. She closed her eyes . . .

Saving the Rainforests

Today there are rainforest protection programs in Sweden, Canada, Germany, the United States, Great Britain and Costa Rica; these programs are saving thousands of acres of rainforest from being destroyed. For more information, you can write to the nearest office of the World Wildlife Fund.

Tropical Rainforests

Tropical rainforests are dense green jungles, where ferns grow as tall as trees, and vines are as thick as ropes. The air is damp and heavy with the smell of leaf mould and flowers.

These forests cover only a small amount of the Earth's surface, but they are home to over half of the plants and animals that live on our planet. There are so many species that even destroying a few hectares of land can wipe out a whole population (in one forest in Costa Rica, the entire breeding range of one species of wasp can be found in an area the size of an average bathroom).

All over the world, rainforests are being cut or burned to make room for grazing land for cattle. For the people who live near the rainforests, cutting down the forests for farmland seems like the only way they can improve their lives and feed their families. But in fact, these forests are more valuable left standing, as a source of fruit and rubber, than being cut for wood and grazing land.

The trees in these rainforests are so old, and the ecosystem they are part of is so complex, that they will never be the same again, even if they are allowed to grow back. In the meantime, because the forests are being destroyed, many birds and animals are losing their homes, including northern birds that spend the winters there. Some of them may become extinct. The soil that was held in place by the roots of the trees is being washed away by the heavy rains, and floods are caused. Not only that, but these huge trees are an important source of the Earth's oxygen; by cutting so many of them we could be making the whole world hotter and drier.

In the last 100 years, half of all the world's tropical rainforests have been destroyed. About 20 hectares (50 acres) are still being destroyed every minute. Scientists believe that by the year 2000, one wildlife species will become extinct every hour.

8

In Your Own Backyard

. . . and hit the earth with a soft rustle.

Samantha's eyes blinked open. The red patch was still there, but it was different. It wasn't a fire at all, it was a red bird, lying in two tiny claw-like hands. The hands belonged to Ms. Phoebe Merganser, wearing her funny black cloak, standing in her own backyard beside her birdfeeder, staring at Samantha with her bright beady eyes.

Samantha gazed around her. Everything was suddenly *smaller*. The trees were no longer enormous leafy palaces, the houses were no longer gigantic castles. At her feet—her very own feet, in her own dirty running shoes with the laces coming undone!—at her feet was Furball, no longer a hideous fang-toothed monster but a sweet, harmless-looking pussycat. She rubbed herself against Samantha's legs as if happy to welcome her home. Samantha felt her shoulders. The wings were gone.

"How did we get back here?" said Samantha. "Did we fly?"

"Fly?" said Phoebe Merganser. "Little girl, have you no respect for your elders? What would a respectable woman like myself be doing flying through the air? Unless you're trying to tell me you think I'm an old witch!" Despite her severe tone of voice, her eyes twinkled. "In any case," she added, "flying's for the birds!"

Earth Day

Every year, on April 22, environmental and wildlife organizations recognize Earth Day—a day set aside to celebrate the earth's ecosystem. The first Earth Day was observed in 1970. Now 1 billion people take part all over the world.

Celebrate Earth Day with your class. Plan special wildlife projects, organize a birdwatching expedition, plant a bird garden in your schoolyard, have a letter-writing bee, or join a naturalist organization.

With that she lifted her hands, and the Cardinal flapped its wings groggily and then fluttered up into a tree. It had only been stunned. Samantha felt very happy that it wasn't dead.

"Were you really a crow?" said Samantha. "And may I come and help you feed the birds, tomorrow?"

"I, a crow?" said Phoebe Merganser. "The idea! You might as well go about saying that you were once a Scarlet Tanager! As for feeding the birds— why don't you put up a birdfeeder in your own backyard? I can show you how to do it."

Birdfeeders

You can make birdfeeders from wood, old milk cartons, onion bags, plastic containers and bottles. To make one of the simplest feeders, just spread peanut butter or lard on a pine cone or a short length of dead tree branch (the more holes and bumps on the branch, the better). Roll the branch or cone in birdseed and hang it on a tree or bush.

Feeding birds gives you a chance to get to know individual birds and observe them up close. But once you start feeding birds in the winter, you should continue until spring (take special care to fill your feeders right after a snowstorm). Birds will start to count on you for food, and if there are no other feeders nearby, they may starve if you suddenly stop feeding them.

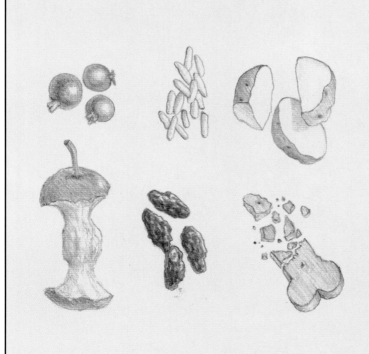

Leftovers for Birds

Some birds also like leftovers, and they'll eat more than stale bread crusts. Here are some things you can try putting out for them:
- *boiled potatoes*
- *crumbled dog biscuits*
- *raw or boiled rice*
- *oatmeal*
- *coconut*
- *lettuce and celery leaves*
- *raisins*
- *apple and pear cores, fruit pits and berries*

Christmas for the Birds

After Christmas, recycle your old Christmas tree for the birds. Stand it in the backyard and hang peanut butter-filled pine cones, strings of popcorn, peanuts in the shell, cranberries, or even stale breadcrusts.

If you have a number of leftover trees at your school, create a "brush-pile" grove of trees in a corner of the schoolground.

"What are you up to out there?" asked Samantha's father the next day. "And where are you going with my shovel?"

"That's to dig a hole for the birdfeeder pole," said Samantha. "We're going to have a birdbath, too. Kerry from across the street is coming over to help, and Ms. Phoebe Merganser is showing us the best place to put it. By the way, we'll need some birdseed."

"Who decided all this?" said her father. "Who is this Phoebe What's-Her-Name? Nobody ever tells me anything!"

"I did, at breakfast time, but you weren't listening," said Samantha. "You were reading the paper and grumbling."

"What put all these bird ideas into your head?" said her father, laughing.

"You did," said Samantha. "Remember how you're always saying, *That's for the birds*? Well, this *is* for the birds. But it's for the rest of us, too."

Index